A Weakness For Men
by Jill Williams

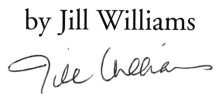

Woodley & Watts
MONTREAL • SEDONA • TAOS

www. woodley-watts.com

ISBN 0-9732870-0-4

ACKNOWLEDGMENTS

The following poems have appeared in print:

Filling The Void — *Heliotrope*, Volume 6
Beginnings — *RIVERRUN*, Summer 1999
My Love For You Is Now A Cloudless Sky
— *Romance 2000*, Wings Of Dawn Press
Middles (formerly titled "Keeping The Middle From Sagging")
— *NEW ENGLAND WRITERS' NETWORK*, Spring 2000
Endings — *RIVERRUN*, Summer, 1999
Overheard On Commercial Drive (formerly titled "The Artist And The Poet") — *The Twisted Quill*, Spring 2000

I would also like to thank Robert Campbell, Portlin Cochise, Lance Eastman, Peter Higginson and Marg Nelson for their support and editorial suggestions.

Author photo : Gordon Glanz
Designer : Sylvain Leblanc

Aug. 2, 2004

For Suzy —

A fellow song-writer!

May the music of

words ring loud in

your heart!

Jill 😊

CONTENTS

GLOSSARY OF POETIC TERMS

BALLADE: Fixed form consisting of three seven or eight-line stanzas using no more than three recurrent rhymes with an identical refrain after each stanza and a closing envoi (coda) repeating the rhymes of the last four lines of the stanza.

KYRIELLE: Popular poetic form originating in France and dating back to the middle ages. The word Kyrielle is derived from a part of the church liturgy, the kyrie eleison. It is written in quatrains (four line stanzas) which include a refrain (repeat line, phrase or word) as the last line, and each line has eight syllables.

LIMERICK: Humorous verse form of five chiefly anapestic lines of which one, two and five are of three feet and lines three and four are of two feet, with a rhyme scheme of aabba.

LIGHT VERSE: Term applied to a great variety of poems that use an ordinary speaking voice and a relaxed manner to treat their subjects gaily, or playfully, or with a good — natured satire. Its subjects may be serious or petty; the defining quality is the tone of voice used and the attitude of the lyric or narrative speaker towards the subject.

PANTOUM: Poem in a fixed form, consisting of a varying number of 4-line stanzas with lines rhyming alternately; the second and fourth lines of each stanza are repeated to form the first and third lines of the succeeding stanza, with the first and third lines of the first stanza forming the second and fourth of the last stanza, but in reverse order, so that the opening and closing lines of the poem are identical.

PARADELLE: Four six-line stanzas in which the first and second lines, as well as the third and fourth lines of the first three stanzas, must be identical. The fifth and sixth lines, which traditionally resolve these stanzas, must use all the words from the preceding stanzas and only those words. Similarly, the final stanza must use every word from all the preceding stanzas and only those words.

RONDEAU: Fixed form used mostly in light or witty verse, usually consisting of fifteen octo-or decasyllabic lines in three stanzas, with only two rhymes used throughout. A word or words from the first part of the first line are used as a (usually unrhymed) refrain ending the second and third stanzas, so the rhyme scheme is aabba aabR aabbaR.

RONDEL: Variation of the rondeau in which the first two lines of the first stanza are repeated as the last two lines of the second and third stanzas, thus a rhyme scheme of Abba abAB abbaA(B).

SONNET: Fixed form consisting of fourteen lines of five-foot iambic verse. The rhyme schemes vary according to the type of sonnet, i.e. Shakespearean (abab, cdcd, efef, gg), Spenserian (abab bcbc cdcd ee), Petrarchan (abba abba and a sestet of two additional rhyme sounds which may be variously arranged), Terza Rima (aba, bcb, cdc, etc.).

TRIOLET: Poem or stanza of eight lines in which the first line is repeated as the fourth and seventh lines, and the second line as the eighth, with a rhyme scheme of ABaAabAB.

VILLANELLE: Set form of nineteen lines; five, three line stanzas and a concluding four line stanza, using only two rhymes. The first and third lines rhyme throughout, as do the middle lines of each stanza. The first and third lines become the refrain of alternate stanzas.

INTRODUCTION:
IN DEFENSE OF FORMAL POETRY

I was raised in New England around a
bunch of tight-lipped, tight-assed Yankees.
But not before developing a taste for formal
verse. My heroines were Edna St. Vincent
Millay and Dorothy Parker, two ladies
whose relationships with men were used
and reused to their creative advantage.
It may be out of style now but there are still
those of us (e.g. Diane Thiel and Wendy
Cope) who aren't put off by the rigors of
thinking and writing in meter. I maintain
that iambic and trochaic rhythms are as
natural as a heartbeat. We grow up on
nursery rhymes. We're taught to memorize
poems that scan. Aside from the sheer
enjoyment of pouring out and purging my
emotions within the prescribed structure of
a sonnet or a villanelle, these forms allow
me to be verbally acrobatic and vulnerable
at the same time. If you absolutely detest
formal poetry, I'd advise you not to read
this book. But if you can suspend poetic
prejudice, you might actually like it.
On the previous page, I have included a
"Glossary Of Poetic Terms." It explains the
rules and rhyme schemes of the forms I've
used. Would that love affairs were as easy
to adapt to as poetic structures!

BIOPOEMS

Before I begin my quest for male companionship, it's time for a little personal history. I had one sister four years older than me, an alcoholic mother, a workaholic father and a couple of short-lived dogs that didn't last any longer than the maids my dad imported from Nassau every year. Cooking for our family would have driven anyone nuts. My father was always on a diet. My mother never was. We all liked different foods and fought vigorously about what we would and wouldn't eat. I coped then as I do now. By writing. My first "book" was published by the next door neighbor's son who had just gotten a printing press for Christmas. It was called "The Girl And The Gashopper." (They didn't have SpellCheck back then.) After that came an illustrated tale about "Tubby, The Penguin." I wrote songs. I made up ballets. I even taught my father how to play "I've Got A Loverly Bunch Of Coconuts" on the piano. Still, it was nothing like "Ozzie And Harriet." Not even close.

Family Ties

Those ties were broken in my troubled youth
As I stood stiff, jaw clenched and posture proud.
I claimed my independence long and loud
From anything that smacked of being couth.
Or had the ring of some parental truth.
I wore my hatred like a body shroud.
A trouble-maker hoping for a crowd,
The alien antithesis of Ruth.
And still I seek approval from his grave,
Those gentle words my father left unsaid.
If only I might find a wand to wave
To rouse this sullen man from playing dead.
"You know I didn't mean to misbehave."
The breezes sigh. A lily shakes its head.

5

A Sister's Regret

I've always been ashamed of home somehow.
The sibling fights that never seemed to end.
But it's too late to beg her pardon now.

The sister I would taunt and call "a cow!"
She tried to be my tutor and my friend.
I've always been ashamed of home somehow.

And so I left. I took a freedom vow.
If only I had changed that nomad trend.
But it's too late. To beg her pardon now

would no more shed the death mask from her brow
than make those fences easier to mend.
I've always been ashamed of home somehow.

No student, I, of Father God or Tao.
I specialized in acts that would offend.
But it's too late to beg her pardon now.

Or thank her for the rancor she'd allow,
Those rocky times when I refused to bend.
I've always been ashamed of home somehow.
But it's too late to beg her pardon now.

Pantoum For My Mother

You told me having babies made you fat.
You swore you nearly died when I drew breath.
No matter what, I will remember that
Long after I forget your date of death.

You swore you nearly died when I drew breath,
That I was both your greatest joy and curse.
Long after I forget your date of death,
I will remember you — and feel much worse.

That I was both your greatest joy and curse.
It's something mothers never ought to say.
I will remember you — and feel much worse
For having stood so firmly in your way.

It's something mothers never ought to say
In jest. Or as they smoke a cigarette.
For having stood so firmly in your way,
I've paid with sobs that left my pillow wet.

There'll be no wee ones waiting for my touch.
No tender toddlers. I'll make sure of that!
You didn't really want me very much.
You told me having babies made you fat.

I Only Eat One Meal A Day

I only eat one meal a day
It keeps me trim and thinner.
Let others stuff the pain away

With crêpes Suzette and cheese soufflé.
I save myself for dinner.
I only eat one meal a day.

"How odd!" the larger ladies say.
They treat me like a sinner.
Let others stuff the pain away

By choosing cake and not sorbet,
Two chins to chide each grinner.
I only eat one meal a day.

I simply will not fill my tray
And praise the pizza-spinner.
Let others stuff the pain away

With brandied four-star peach flambé.
Food needn't be the winner.
I only eat one meal a day.
Let others stuff the pain away.

*The following two poems introduce two of the first "men" in my life.
For better or worse they were not the last. They also introduce a form
created by Poet Laureate Billy Collins. A paradelle (combination
"paradox" and "villanelle") consists of four six-line stanzas. The first
two lines of each stanza repeat themselves; the last two lines must use
all the words from the previous lines. The final stanza is made up of
all the words from the rest of the poem.*

Groton, Connecticut: 1956

I was 13 and, boy oh boy, did I have a crush.
I was 13 and, boy oh boy, did I have a crush.
On the lifeguard. What? I dunno his name.
On the lifeguard. What? I dunno his name.
Boy, did I have — His name? #13 Lifeguard.
What a crush on the boy! And I was, oh, I dunno—

I got my period that summer.
I got my period that summer.
How I bled red on our beach towel.
How I bled red on our beach towel.
My summer bled on. How red I got!
That beach period? Our towel? I—

He saw and then went snickering away.
He saw and then went snickering away.
Into his waves I jumped, cheeks aflame.
Into his waves I jumped, cheeks aflame.
Saw his snickering waves and cheeks.
Aflame, I jumped. Away into then he went.

Crush the lifeguard and his snickering cheeks!
He saw summer aflame on a beach.
What was his name? "Boy 13?"

9

Bled red, I did, on our towel.
I jumped. I went away. I — Oh, boy. I dunno.
My period and then waves. (How have I got into that?)

Dennis, Massachusetts: 1963

After Mark got mad that lovelier summer day.
After Mark got mad that lovelier summer day,
He cuffed my left ear and my heart went deaf.
He cuffed my left ear and my heart went deaf.
Summer got lovelier after Mark left that day.
My, my. Deaf heart? Cuffed ear? And he went

To Bernardsville and his snooty parents.
To Bernardsville and his snooty parents.
Where servants iron those Brooks Brothers shirts.
Where servants iron those Brooks Brothers shirts.
Iron parents. And those brothers, Snooty and Brooks.
His shirts to *where,* servants? Bernardsville!

I was at The Cape. Glad to be rid of the bastard.
I was at The Cape. Glad to be rid of the bastard.
Suntanned, of course. But I couldn't hear much.
Suntanned, of course. But I couldn't hear much.
The much-bastard was suntanned, of course.
But rid of glad, I hear. To be at The Cape? I couldn't.

After I was cuffed, those Bernardsville brothers
And his snooty parents went to The Cape. Servants?
Glad. Rid of shirts to iron. My sun-tanned heart
Couldn't hear much. And he left my deaf ear.
Where that summer day? At the brooks.
But I got lovelier, Mark.(Of course, be mad. Bastard.)

Time passes whether we want it to or not. Even if my heart still beats in teenage rhythms and I continue to thrill to the sound of a deep male voice, the mirror is there to remind me....

Falling In Love After 50

It's not the same as when you're twenty-five
And full of dreams that don't make any sense.
You haven't had a lifetime to survive
And be replaced by youth's omnipotence.
Your confidence is shaken to its roots
Like branches when the wind begins to buck.
You feel too old to buy designer boots.
You'd rather spend the money on a tuck.
And what of him, your partner in this folly.
Is he as deadly insecure as you?
I think not. By his attitude — so jolly —
He knows his dating days are far from through.
While you know this could be your last affair.
A fact that makes new dreams too much to bear.

Coping With Death

I loved the man so very much.
But when the cancer came along,
I turned to tennis as a crutch.
To help me cope; to keep me strong.

But when the cancer came along,
I chose this serve and volley game.
To help me cope; to keep me strong.
Some said I should be filled with shame.

I chose this serve and volley game
It gave me courage, self-respect.
Some said I should be filled with shame.
I wonder now in retrospect.

It gave me courage, self-respect.
I hid my heart on courts of clay.
I wonder now in retrospect.
What force could keep the pain away?

I hid my heart on courts of clay.
I turned to tennis as a crutch.
No matter what my critics say,
I loved the man so very much.

MOVING TO VANCOUVER

MOVING TO VANCOUVER

I was deeply involved — I called it "love" at the time — with a man whose past both repelled and fascinated me. He'd spent the majority of his life behind bars. Chino. San Quentin. Folsom. Nothing like a law-breaker to turn a girl on! He eventually went straight, cleaned up his heroin habit and then died on me. After those final months of care giving, I had nothing left but a big gaping hole in my heart. I tried being brave. But every street reminded me of him, of the roller coaster ride we'd shared for four and a half incredibly crazy years. I had to get away.

Someplace New

Exactly how I got here I don't know.
It had to do with Edward slowly dying.
I needed someplace new to let him go.

A change of scene to heal and help me grow,
To stop my hollow chest from always sighing.
Exactly how I got here I don't know.

I'd reached a flat, impassable plateau,
Where breathing was the same to me as crying.
I needed someplace new to let him go.

Where pain and loss would melt away like snow
And hope might rise again like eagles flying.
Exactly how I got here, I don't know.

I did a lot of pacing to-and-fro
Debating if this trip would be worth trying.
I needed someplace new to let him go.

The day I came the clouds were thick and low
But even so, my sorrow started drying.
Exactly how I got here, I don't know.
I needed someplace new to let him go.

I fell in love with Stanley Park. The seawall with its odd assortment
of roller-bladers, beach bums and well-dressed pan handlers. One lady
wheeled two geese — dressed in blue and white checkered caps and
bibs — around the park in a baby carriage. And the natural beauty
left me speechless! Those tall, graceful trees. Eagles flying overhead.
My favorite statue was of Vancouver's Harry Winston Jerome. To me,
he looked though he'd take off any second. When I first started walk-
ing the wall, I couldn't get over how no one seemed to mind the rain.
"Spitting" was the term they used. I soon learned that umbrellas were
to be carried but never opened. Not if you were a true Vancouverite.
What a special place. I was determined to make it my own personal
paradise.

Harry Winston Jerome, Athlete Of The Century

Why the odd glint in your eye!
Thinking of racing the breeze?
Please, Harry. Let it blow by.
Statues have lead in their knees.

Thinking of racing the breeze?
Don't even try to compete.
Statues have lead in their knees.
Bronze doesn't lighten one's feet.

Don't even try to compete.
Leave former glories alone.
Bronze doesn't lighten one's feet,
Better stay put on that stone.

Leave former glories alone.
Keep those arms frozen and poised.
Better stay put on that stone.
Best you inspire young boys.

Breezes can sometimes stir quarrels.
Please, Harry. Let them blow by.
I say "Rest well on your laurels."
Why the odd glint in your eye!

Spirits Of Stanley Park

They move in silence through the human throng
And guide the roller-bladers through the dark.
Despite the fact they're dead they still belong
To certain well-placed benches the park.
The names and dedications seem to fit,
From poetry, to "We all miss you so!"
It matters not where you decide to sit,
A spirit's at your back that you don't know.
His loved ones are recovering by now.
Some days are fun, some days are grey and grim.
Ye ghosts of Stanley Park, come take a bow
And shine your phantom light on each new limb.
Without your presence we might never see
A preview of our own mortality.

I met Roy while playing tennis. He had a thick French accent, too much hair on his back and a sex drive that wouldn't quit. But he cooked. And he sewed. And I figured I'd get used to his arrogance.

Novocain

I've found a way to numb my pain.
His droning voice dulls me to sleep.
At night it feels like novocain.
I've found a way to numb my pain.
He wears brown suits and one gold chain,
And boasts of things bought "on the cheap."
I've found a way to numb my pain
His droning voice dulls me to sleep.

Proposal In The Rose Garden

On bended knee, he begs to wed
With longing in those eyes. And dread.
  His lustful needs, so all-consuming,
  Shake the roses round him blooming.
"Shh!" they whisper. "Use your head!"

Their perfect petals drenched in red
Are wounded by the words he's said.
  Can't he sense the end is looming
               On bended knee?

These roses know when love is dead.
When someone is obsessed instead.
  She turns him down and leaves, assuming
  He'll be hurt at first. Then fuming.
The flowers cheer. He's made his bed
               On bended knee.

Filling The Void

Who will it be ignites these pheromones?
Which tarnished knight with ever-hopeful bones
Will take my hand, as dark replaces light,
And make me want to stay with him all night?
"Come on," he'll urge, "We'll give the moon a thrill.
Let's lay a blanket over by that hill
And shake the summer stars out of the sky.
Forget the past,our love will keep us high!"
Where is this Lancelot? Does he exist?
This dreamer who will take me by my wrist
And waltz me round the world just one more time.
For him, how old I am won't be a crime.
O promise me he's there or I'll expire.
For what is left if one can't feel desire.

The following poem requires some background. I had by this time decided to make Vancouver my permanent home. Sadly enough, the only way to make this happen was to marry a Canadian. I'd worked out a plan whereby I'd pay ten thousand dollars to anyone who would help me become a Landed Immigrant. Five hundred up front, the rest upon divorce. Art and I met in George's Café on Denman Street. He had a ruddy, alcoholic's complexion and a ragged Joe Cocker voice. He told me he'd had a problem with cocaine but that was all in the past now — thanks to "A Course In Miracles." A sane woman would have paid for the coffee and left. Instead, I married him.

October 24, 1989

The wedding was perfection, that's for sure.
   I hardly knew a single person there.
I wore a chiffon skirt and played demure
   With autumn posies scattered through my hair.
   The groom stood proud. His shoulders, straight and square.
Despite that penguin suit, he was a "hunk".
   And at the party, glasses in mid-air,
We toasted 'To true love!' and then got drunk.

My motives, I'll admit, were less than pure.
   A trumped up marriage seemed a bit unfair.
But as I scrawled my newest signature,
   I didn't think the government would care.
   No sex. That was our deal. I made him swear.
I'd take the bed. The couch is where he'd bunk.
   A week went by. He bought some wine to share.
We toasted 'To true love!' and then got drunk.

What once was cut-and-dried becomes obscure.
   He tells me he no longer feels despair.
He wants to wed for real. I am his cure.

"I love you madly. Love *me,* if you dare!"
I put him off. That sets him on a tear.
"You lying little bitch! You sneaky skunk!"
His insults are too much for me to bear.
I toast "To truer love!" and then get drunk.

L'Envoi
To you, it must seem sadly insecure.
I should have said "Adieu!" and shipped my trunk.
But I was charmed by Canada's allure.
Let's toast her coastal shores and then get drunk.

Postscript

I'm living with another man by now.
He's pouring boiling water for our tea.
The phone rings. "Art is dead." But when and how!
(I wonder why his brother's telling me?)
We'd been divorced. He moved to Dawson Creek.
Instinctively I shut the window shades.
"He died of…" I can barely hear him speak.
"From complications brought about by AIDS."
I thank him for informing me of this
And offer deep condolences as well.
My lover leans in closer for a kiss.
"Not now!" I snap. "Bad timing. Can't you tell?"
I catch my breath and eye the stars above.
We'd come damn close but never did make love.

PENDER ISLAND

By this time, I had begun teaching a creative writing course at a local community college. Aside from inspiring me to pen some light verses about how to get published, it also introduced me to my next "great love." The minute Laird walked into that classroom, there was a connection. For the next decade, he would play numerous roles: talented student, worshipful lover, disillusioned husband, recovering alcoholic, obsessive ex, business partner. Even to this day, I know I will never get him completely out of my system. Like writing.

Beginnings

Think of your opening sentence
The way you'd want someone to kiss.
Make it so strong and appealing
That readers say, "This one can't miss!"

Work on the opening chapter
By heaping on more of the same.
Nothing sells books (or affection)
Like wondering who'll win the game.

My Love For You Is Now A Cloudless Sky

My love for you is now a cloudless sky,
Without the hint of rainy days to come.
And even if there were our hearts would hum.
Yes, we're too new at this to want to cry
When thunderheads, like horses, canter by.
Their rumble may leave other lovers glum,
Afraid of tender feelings going numb.
Not us! We're still on ground that's safe and dry.
We haven't yet encountered any storms.
Or light'ning flashes right before the blast.
So far there've been no angry nimbus swarms
To block the sun and make us overcast.
New passion comes in such amorphous forms.
I only pray this cloudlessness will last.

I Wish I'd Been A Virgin

I wish I'd been a virgin when we met
With lips so pure that even gods would blush.
As innocent as Shakespeare's Juliet,
My love would give us both a holy rush.

With lips so pure that even gods would blush,
I'd tentatively stroke your friendly beard.
Our love would give us both a holy rush,
Hushed moments to be savored and revered.

I'd tentatively stroke your friendly beard,
And give myself completely to this night,
Hushed moments to be savored and revered.
A kiss, a touch, so much untapped delight!

I'd give myself completely to this night.
The first time we were lovers, you and I.
A kiss, a touch, so much untapped delight!
Why is it I am suddenly so shy?

Perhaps because I know I'll never be
As innocent as Shakespeare's Juliet.
I wonder. Are there others just like me?
I wish I'd been a virgin when we met.

We honeymooned at one of the Canadian Gulf Islands — North Pender — in a darling little cabin on Clam Bay. The bathroom was located about a hundred yards away. Early that first morning, as I headed over to relieve myself, the whoosh of bald eagle wings jolted me awake. When I came back and told Laird about it, he was consumed with envy. "How come all the really great moments happen to you and not me?" It wasn't the kindest thing to say to a new bride.

Middles

I compare mid-story lag
With boredom in a marriage.
Cinderella trapped inside
Prince Charming's musty carriage.
Writers use a plot outline
To keep their tale in motion.
Would that outlines worked in life
To jump start lost devotion!

Quintet

We spread our feast beside Deer Lake,
With silences and bread to break.
Fresh cold cuts placed so gracefully.
Five meant for him, five meant for me.

We spoke of this. We spoke of that.
We joked about our growing fat
And spread the crisps with too much Brie.
Five meant for him, five meant for me.

But then, as night ate up the skies,
We could not help but share more lies.
How much we loved! How faithfully!
Five meant for him, five meant for me.

Endings

Aesop? The man was a master!
His morals had lessons to teach.
Now he'd be thought a disaster
Since readers detest those who preach.

Still, there are some rules we follow
The hero must live by his wits.
Villains' emotions ring hollow
And justice is doled out in bits.

So when your words start to wander,
Stick close to the point and don't stray.
Love's not about what lies yonder.
It's making the best of today.

Deciding Factor

I've all the money I need.
Too bad it threatens your maleness.
Foolish to think we'd succeed.
I've all the money I need.
Bore me no more about greed
How it breeds nothing but staleness.
I've all the money I need.
Too bad it threatens your maleness.

From Far Away

From far away and yet so near
I still can feel his touch from here,
And sense how much that knee joint aches
Despite the constant pills he takes.
I can't believe it's been a year.

We fell apart, undone by fear
That wore a mask of false good cheer.
It seems unreal. Like stardust flakes
           From far away.

And yet I shed a sudden tear
And will my pain to disappear.
I raise a fist. It quails and shakes.
"Must I repeat these same mistakes?"
The moon says "No!" Her answer clear
           From far away.

After Laird and I broke up, I moved to Pender Island. It gave me a place far enough away from Vancouver's mainland to lick my wounds, listen to sad music and replenish those fantasy-dreams of one day finding Prince Valiant.

Orcas Crossing

I thought I'd seen most all the roadway signs.
Those yellow squares, the silhouettes in black.
From "Kids At Play" to "Don't Cross Double Lines."
But this sign took me totally aback.

Those yellow squares, the silhouettes in black.
An outline showed much more than words could say.
Yes, this sign took me totally aback.
It warned of "Orcas Crossing" at Thieves' Bay.

An outline showed much more than words could say:
One leaping whale, then wavy lines of sea.
It warned of "Orcas Crossing" at Thieves' Bay.
The locals claim the pod shows up at three.

One leaping whale, then wavy lines of sea.
Perhaps today I'll view this wondrous sight.
The locals claim the pod shows up at three.
"They're coming now! In living black and white!"

I've read of hairpin turns and roads that dip.
From "Kids At Play" to "Don't Cross Double Lines."
But till I took that Pender Island trip,
I thought I'd seen most all the roadway signs.

Penance At The Ferry Terminal

It's Tuesday after Easter. Praise the Lord!
I'm resurrected, eager to return.
Don't say there's no more room for me on board.

There has to be. I need a quick reward
For all my pseudo-worshipful concern.
It's Tuesday after Easter. Praise the Lord!

My hostess has been properly adored.
Despite the meals she couldn't help but burn.
Don't say there's no more room for me on board.

Just squeeze me in beside that blue Accord
I like the bumper sticker: "Save A Fern!"
It's Tuesday after Easter. Praise the Lord!

Here's twenty bucks. That's all I can afford.
A meager bribe I beg you not to spurn.
Don't say there's no more room for me on board.

I need my faith in miracles restored.
Please take another "look-see" in the stern.
It's Tuesday after Easter. Praise the Lord!
Don't say there's no more room for me on board.

Pender Island Wave

They wave at you on Pender as you walk,
Their rusty pick-ups nearly gone to pot.
This gesture saves a ton of idle talk
And tells you who is liked and who is not.
For those who're new and still impressed by deer,
A single waving finger will suffice.
Two fingers? As a gesture, it's sincere.
A warmer welcome to this paradise.
In time, some wave at you with fingers three.
A signal meant to melt the hardest heart.
Alas, it hasn't happened yet to me.
I'm up to two, which seems a hopeful start.
I'll get there someday. Maybe in the spring
(The same time turkey vultures learn to sing.)

Heading East

I was ready to begin my quest for love again. But not ready to admit it publicly. My friends all wished me well. They told me where to stay, what to do, who to phone when I got there. "Have a wonderful trip," they said, waving a little too brightly as I took off in my battered Honda Civic. It gets harder and harder on friends when they see how desperately finding a mate matters. I could just imagine them comparing notes, asking the same tired question: "Who will she force on us this time?"

Spruce Meadows Horseshow

On Friday, it is freeze-your-nose-off cold.
I haven't packed a jacket or a coat.
I see the tents where foreign foods are sold.
And head on over, clutching at my throat.
A café latte brings me some relief.
But still the numbness travels up my toes.
There's only one solution to this grief:
I'll have to buy more costly winter clothes.
Next morning, it is sweat-your-shirt-off hot.
I haven't brought a single pair of shorts.
Instead, a brand new parka's all I've got
To cover me while Spain's top stallion snorts.
Spruce Meadows. Such an elegant affair!
For me, it's meant new duds I'll never wear.

Welcome To Winnipeg

It's dead-ass cold. Or else there's flies,
Depending on the time of year.
The choices stink. Like day-old beer.
And no one wants to advertise
This unremitting compromise.
For those who must relocate here,
It's dead-ass cold. Or else there's flies,
Depending on the time of year.

But who am I to criticize
What Manitobans hold so dear.
They don't need me to foster fear
Or question why, beneath flat skies,
It's dead-ass cold. Or else there's flies....

During the rare moments when I was romantically unencumbered, I poured myself into being creative. I wrote a musical for the Fringe Festival, a book of poetry and numerous newspaper articles. Still, I hungered for a mate. Someone I could "grow old with gracefully." But I had my standards: a.) He couldn't be gay; b.) He couldn't be a redneck; and c.) He couldn't be more than three years younger than me. As luck would have it, Leland fell into two of these categories.

"Ontario Affairio"

Toronto's where we met, a charming spot.
It's ethnic sections clear and well-defined.
He loved me true. And then he loved me not.

This lanky lad who claimed he was a Scot.
Who grew up foster-raised and unrefined.
Toronto's where we met, a charming spot.

He played his jazz and smoked his home-grown pot
And swore he'd left the harder stuff behind.
He loved me true. And then he loved me not.

We'd amble west of Yonge. (He shopped a lot.)
He wore a diamond earring he'd designed.
Toronto's where we met, a charming spot.

Except when sudden heat waves make it hot,
Or fights erupt and someone gets maligned.
He loved me true. And then he loved me not.

Our union had a *film noire* kind of plot.
His face was smooth while mine seemed spider-lined.
Toronto's where we met, a charming spot.
He loved me true. And then he loved me not.

Naked Men With Muscles

I found them after we had just had sex:
His stash of body-building magazines.
Great-looking guys with bulging arms and pecs.
I bit my tongue. We'd had enough bad scenes.
If only they'd been empty cans of Beck's.
Or girlie posters filched from old latrines.
I bit my tongue. What could I really say?
I knew his love would swing the other way.

Leland's Scottish Auntie

"About your auntie. What'd she think of me?"
He seems evasive, awkward with the truth.
"Oh well," I say. "We had a pleasant tea."
"Want more?" He jumps up quickly from our booth.

He seems evasive, awkward with the truth.
I know it's wrong to push. I never should.
"Want more?" He jumps up quickly from our booth.
It's clear by now her "praise" was not that good.

I know it's wrong to push. I never should.
With Lee, the more you push the less you learn.
It's clear by now her "praise" was not that good.
My cheeks flush red, a slow and steady burn.

With Lee, the more you push the less you learn.
But this is something I cannot resist.
My cheeks flush red, a slow and steady burn.
"Just tell me what she said. I won't be pissed."

"Long in the tooth," he snaps. "It means you're old."
"Oh well," I say. "We had a pleasant tea."
"We did," he lies. I wish I'd not been told
About his aunt and what she thought of me.

Without Any Men

I've given up smoking and drinking.
I've given up sleeping till nine.
I'm working on negative thinking
And trying to change how I dine.
I've given up many resentments
Or channeled them well with a pen.
So why can't I find my contentments
Alone and without any men?

I've managed to keep my own dentures.
My bosom retains its soft curve.
I've played out all kinds of adventures
With courage and humor and verve.
But still, when the john seat is down now,
I get this unbearable yen.
So why must I walk around town now
Alone and without any men?

It's something that I must get over.
This feeling of failure and loss.
I don't need more rolls in the clover
I'm up to my elbows in moss!
Forget about all and resplendent.
I care not for "who, where or when."
I'll conquer this life. Independent.
Alone and without any men.

MONTREAL

"Just For Laughs" is an annual comedy festival that takes place in Montreal every summer. I was lucky enough to get a last-minute ticket and thus began my next close encounter.

Just For Laughs

I'd seen it on TV a million times.
This festival where "funny" wins applause
And comics do their bits without a pause.
One hates his wife. Another speaks in rhymes.
A kinkster shares his whip-on-leather crimes.
Comediennes , like felines, bare their claws.
And balding fat guys really milk their flaws.
There's lemons in the bunch. But mostly limes.
So here I sit. Alone. In Montréal.
That is, until the man beside me speaks:
"You have a hearty laugh for one so small."
(Nobody's tried to pick me up for weeks.)
I look at him and giggle back. "You think?"
Then just for laughs we head out for a drink.

Secret Cards

We counted cobblestones and then we stopped.
Place Jacques-Cartier was full of life and song
I laughed and said, "Those comics can't be topped!"
He took my hand and winked, "You could be wrong."

Place Jacques-Cartier was full of life and song.
It was as if a circus came to town.
Again, he took my hand. "You could be wrong."
We found a *bon terasse* and settled down.

It was as if a circus came to town,
I liked this man. I liked him right away.
We found a *bon terasse* and settled down.
We had some secret cards left yet to play.

I liked this man. I liked him right away.
He poured his *bière* and blew away the fizz.
We had some secret cards left yet to play.
I knew my own. But what, pray tell, were his?

"You looked so very lovely in that hall."
I laughed and said, "Those comics can't be topped!"
He kissed my cheek. "*Let's conquer Montréal!*"
We counted cobblestones and then we stopped.

Casino de Montréal

Three thousand noisy slot machines.
  The air feels full of love and hate.
I ask my friend what this all means.
  He has a simple truth to state:
  "One's life is either small or great.
Depending on one's fate. Or pride.
  I place my chips and simply wait
Until the wheel is on my side."

The bettors have their strict routines.
  Some sit alone. Some bring a date.
I watch the machos and the queens.
  They're here to win and celebrate.
  And so am I. "Place ten on eight!"
My friend's a mentor, fan and guide.
  Won't know if he's the perfect mate
Until the wheel is on my side.

This *bon vivant* in tails or jeans
  Would make most ladies salivate.
From dowagers to young colleens
  His winning ways intoxicate.
  Damn, snake eyes. Does this indicate
It's time for me to stop the ride?
  Or let the chips accelerate
Until the wheel is on my side.

L'Envoi
  "To open wide or shut love's gate."
We'll never answer this debate.
  I'll gamble on. Won't buck the tide.
Until the wheel is on my side.

We had a week of unremitting laughter and romance. I was staying at a hotel on René-Lévesque and should have guessed something was wrong when my lover refused to give me his home phone number. "Use the cell," he'd say. "It's much faster." Obviously, he had something — or someone — to hide. A wife, maybe? I didn't want to believe it. But then I saw them in the supermarket. I could tell by the way they joked over which melon was the ripest that they'd been shopping together for years. I was tempted to follow her down one of the aisles. "Excusez-moi, Madame. Do you know that I'm sleeping with your husband?" She'd probably reply:

Delusions D'une Épouse

Il n'appartiendra jamais à vous.
Dans l'âme, dans le corps et dans l'esprit.
Il est un menteur. Mais entre nous,
Il n'appartiendra jamais à vous.
Je suis né ses enfants, je fais tout.
Je serai toujours ici pour lui.
Il n'appartiendra jamais à vous.
Dans l'âme, dans le corps et dans l'esprit.

A Wife's Delusions

He never will belong to you.
In his soul, or body, or mind.
He lies, I know. But one thing's true:
He never will belong to you.
I've borne his children, seen him through.
Love like mine's not easy to find.
He never will belong to you.
In his soul, or body, or mind.

ATLANTIC CANADA

I'd been corresponding with a fellow who lived in Halifax, Nova Scotia. We'd kept things fairly light, knowing from previous internet connections how disappointing they can be in person. But I hadn't been to eastern Canada and I thought seeing it with someone who was familiar with the countryside would double my enjoyment. I knew better than to expect this stranger, whose smile from his photos was both sexy and sincere, to be my romantic salvation. "Forget that!" I told myself as I waited for him to pick me up at the airport, remembering other men I'd met in this same fashion.

The Riddle of Attraction

Why, tell me why, must the men I *don't* love
　　Gather around me like frogs in a pond?
　　Crowding and croaking their hopes of a bond,
Placing me higher than Heaven above.
What makes them think my hand fits in their glove?
　　Suitors whose faces would break any wand.
　　Why, tell me why, must the men I *don't* love
Gather around me like frogs in a pond?

Then comes the prince I've been day-dreaming of.
　　Nothing I say seems to make him respond.
He'd rather fawn over some busty blonde.
　　I get a handshake. Or even a shove!
　　Why, tell me why, must the men I *don't* love
Gather around me like frogs in a pond?

Perfect Match

He'd said that writing novels was his thing.
　　Unpublished yet. But someday he would be.
His phrases had a literary ring.
　　Like Marcel Proust, Virginia Wolfe. (And me!)
　　A silver-haired professor-by-the-sea
Whose pattern was to love and then detach.
I had this sudden impulse just to flee.
Once more I begged, "Let this one be a match!"

I looked outside beyond the airplane's wing,
　　Expecting yet another Tweedledee.
Afraid of what this face-to-face might bring.
　　No spark, no joy, no instant chemistry
　　He'd try to cop a feel or squeeze a knee.
And there I'd be in some old bramble patch.
　　He'd tease me with "This guided tour ain't free!"
Once more I begged, "Let this one be a match!"

And then I saw him wave. A bell went "Ting!"
　　My outsides and my insides shouted "Whee!"
I felt an urge to kick my heels and sing
　　But didn't dare. Instead, I went to pee.
　　When I returned to Parking Section "B,"
He stood beside a transit buses' hatch.
　　(I made a final frenzied silent plea:)
"Please, God," I said, "Let this one be a match!"

　　　　L'Envoi
What then, you ask. Unfold the mystery!
He drove a public bus. ("Best o' the batch.")
　　My knight in short-sleeved armor turned the key.
And there we were, a far from perfect match.

VANCOUVER REVISITED

Retracing one's steps is often an exercise in futility. Dwelling in the past, glorifying what was instead of what is. But there comes a point when you run out of options. I had reached that point. After many a month (and many a man), I needed to prove that Laird was no longer a clear and present danger in my life. Would I be able to settle down now without secretly hoping we'd bump into each other again and things would be different this time?

Snow Geese On The Wing

I needed this last time to walk the dyke,
To test how far I'd come. (Or maybe not).
Six years can change relationships a lot.
From lustfull need to down and dislike.
I pass an elder pedaling his bike;
And marsh cows, grazing peaceful in one spot;
Some pillared homes with dogs that yap and trot;
And then a map of places one can hike.
I think about the blissful times we had.
Euphoric days, intoxicating nights.
I can't remember now when it turn bad,
Or when we traded tenderness for fights.
I watch a flock of snow geese on the wing.
Their presence is, like love, a fleeting thing.

Overheard On Commercial Drive

They sat outside so he could have a smoke.
   They drank Americanos in the sun.
Each bitching how they hated being broke
   And always eating Big Macs on the run.
   But that was life, and life was mostly fun.
Except for socks with far too many holes
   And smarmy landlords they were forced to shun.
Such is the price one pays for feeding souls.

"I've titled this new piece "The Velvet Cloak."
   The Artist added bits of cinnamon.
They sipped their coffees. Then the Poet spoke
   And later rued the tempest she'd begun.
   "I'm so glad words are what I use to stun
Instead of messy paint and mixing bowls."
   The Artist stormed inside to get a bun.
Such is the price one pays for feeding souls.

When he returned, he had a diet coke
   And murder in his eyes for everyone.
He turned the color of an artichoke
   And jabbed his finger at her like a gun.
   "My talent doesn't need a clever pun.
Or ballade rhymes. I seek much higher goals.
   You write, I paint. There's no comparison!"
Such is the price one pays for feeding souls.

L'Envoi

Dear Muse, how can this argument be won?
They both deserve a hearty round of skoals!
   From Cezanne to the sonnetry of Donne,
Such is the price one pays for feeding souls.

Nitobe Garden

The stillness of this place rings in my mind.
As water falling softly intervenes.
Each bridge has been so carefully designed.
I wonder what "Kasuga style" means?

As water falling softly intervenes,
I watch a giant koi glide through the pond
And wonder what "Kasuga style" means,
As sunlight turns the leaves from green to blonde.

I watch a giant koi glide through the pond.
Five squadron ducklings splash-land into view
As sunlight turns the leaves from green to blonde,
They have their aerobatic drills to do.

Five squadron ducklings splash-land into view,
Their sudden entrance celebrating life.
They have their aerobatic drills to do —
Like household chores between a man and wife.

Nitobe's gifts cannot be praised enough.
Each bridge has been so carefully designed.
Whichever path I chose, stone smooth or rough,
The stillness of this place rings in my mind.

Rock Art Along The Seawall

Why don't they tumble in the sea?
She ponders this while strolling by.
How balance creates mystery.
Like all the deeds in history.
She'll just enjoy this crisp July.
And yet she can't suppress a sigh.
Why don't they tumble in the sea?

Moving to Sedona

After 9-11, I felt I was living in the wrong place at the wrong time. I wanted to be back in the United States. I wanted an American flag decal on my car. I wanted to be able to weep openly every time I heard "The Star-Spangled Banner."

Lions Gate Bridge After 9-11

Majestic bridge from north to south.
Two lions at the harbor's mouth.
For me you were Vancouver's crown.
Until they blew those towers down.

Before, I'd walk the wall and think
What brilliant sunsets bathed in pink!
For me this was the greatest town,
Until they blew those towers down.

And then I heard my own scared voice
"You must return. You have no choice."
I lived to flirt, to play the clown.
Until they blew those towers down.

People ask me, "Why Sedona?" I don't really know. I'm not much into vortexes or psychic phenomenon. And I'd never seen photographs of its famed red rocks jutting out of the earth like castles or cartoon characters. Something just told me it would be a healing place with enough variety to keep my mind and heart happy. I drove down with Karl — another internet acquaintance — who offered to chauffer me, my cat and my car all the way from Seattle, Washington to Flagstaff, Arizona. It was an offer I couldn't refuse. We arrived on December 5th. That first day was fairytale perfect, the rocks dusted with a thin layer of snow. I just knew I'd somehow turned a corner.

Snoopy Rock

His feet seem splayed. He looks asleep, the mutt.
The world could blow apart and on he'd doze.
Unless some climber spiked his beagle nose.
Or Lucy came alive and kicked his butt:
"Who do you think you are?" she'd cry. "King Tut?
I order you to change that lazy pose.
I want to see some wiggle in those toes!
You're much too young to have that big old gut.
Wake up! Right now! It's time to take a run!
You mustn't simply lie there day and night.
You'll burn alive in all that desert sun!
Your coat is turning red instead of white,
Like lobsters boiling in a pot of soup.
You make a better *dog* than rock art, Snoop!"

Two Giant Horse Statues

Their hocks are chrome. Their hooves have locks and keys.
The Trojan soldiers might have mocked these two.
(For sixty-thousand bucks, I wouldn't sneeze.)

And when you see them, prancing in the breeze,
You marvel at the artist's derring-do.
Their hocks are chrome. Their hooves have locks and keys.

Drain covers substitute for equine knees.
One horse's stomach is a junkyard stew.
(For sixty-thousand bucks? Who's gonna sneeze.)

And what a drive-by gimmick, what a tease!
These statues rake in tons of revenue.
Their hocks are chrome. Their hooves have locks and keys.

They look as big and tough as Hercules,
(Without a rusty Maytag peeking through.)
For sixty-thousand bucks, I wouldn't sneeze.

According to a salesgirl named Louise,
The Turquoise Tortoise markets quite a few.
Their hocks are chrome. Their hooves have locks and keys.
(For sixty-thousand bucks, I wouldn't sneeze.)

I still longed for that elusive "silver fox" but the emotional intensity was less. If he came along? Fantastic. If not, I wasn't going to let his absence stop me from experiencing every adventure life has to offer. I'd begun toying with the idea of riding a mule to the bottom of the Grand Canyon and staying overnight at the 80-year-old Phantom Ranch. Who might I interest in such a project?

Peter was the most handsome man I'd ever been with. Wavy gray hair, thin body, perfect features. He had a great sense of humor, too. I remember when he flew out to visit me from Florida that first time — a kind of preview to see if we'd be simpatico enough to mule ride together — he made me laugh right away. He was self-effacing despite his movie star looks. And a superb listener. I was immediately smitten. We'd lie in bed and talk all night. No sex. We'd agreed beforehand to take it slow. I did, however, ask if he could recall the most sensual moment he'd ever had? He told me about a young hooker in Viet Nam.

Remembering Danang

She asks him if he'll buy a girl a drink.
Her almond eyes are soft, her hair waist-long.
She doesn't need to add a special wink.
Or lift the flowered hem of her sarong.
No doubt his Baptist folks would say it's wrong.
The worst of ways a girl can earn her keep.
He listens when she speaks — it's like a song.
"So sorry but I have no place to sleep."
"There's my hotel," he answers, breathing deep.
That night she sets his dormant dreams ablaze.
And as the Asian dawn begins to creep
Beneath the door in muted summer rays,
She takes him by surprise one final time.
So long ago. And still it feels sublime.

We rode the mules in May. His was named Betty, mine Vivian. And we also stopped en route to pay our respects to Moonchild, the sacred white buffalo. It was a memorable five days full of visual delights and aching muscles. But by the end of the trip, Peter had put me in the "just friends" category. So we parted, knowing that what we had shared would always be remembered fondly. For me, it created the following poems:

White Buffalo

They bring the gifts both large and small.
A leather pouch, a painted ball.
   One laughs aloud. One heaves a sigh.
   Another scans the northern sky.
They nod about an early fall.

Compared to most, she isn't tall.
But when her brothers come to call
   She knows her coat's the reason why
            They bring the gifts.

"White buffalo," Lakotas drawl.
"She's here at last to heal us all."
   Three DNA tests do not lie.
   They knew she'd show up, by and by.
A pack of smokes, a beaded shawl,
            They bring the gifts.

On The Way To Phantom Ranch

I had to guide that mule downhill
To prove an ancient truth to me:
That age must never conquer will.
I had to guide that mule downhill,
Despite my lack of riding skill.
Accomplishment sets demons free.
I had to guide that mule downhill
To prove an ancient truth to me.

One Saturday morning I decided to drive to The Grand Hotel in Jerome, Arizona. I'd heard about its ghostly charms, the incredible view. And as I wove my way upward on 89A, past dozens of dedicated cyclists, I was feeling pretty good about being single. Then, for some odd reason, Laird came skulking into my mind. The menu from "The Asylum Restaurant & Lounge" talked about the invisible diners who just might be watching you from a corner....

The Ghost I'd Most Like To Meet

If there's a ghost I'd really like to meet,
   Her given name would be Miss Thelma Mae.
Is she the witch Laird swears she is? Or sweet.
   A southern belle. Naïve. And easy prey.
   I'd love to hear what she might have to say
About the boy she cuddled in her bed
   While Daddy was a soldier far away.
Does Oedipus stop haunting once you're dead?

For sure, my queries might be indiscreet:
   "How friendly were those games you liked to play?
Those times you begged young Laird to rub your feet
   And wore your most revealing negligee.
   You just assumed those actions were okay?
That if he'd felt uneasy, he'd have said.
   So tell me, Thelma. After the decay,
Does Oedipus stop haunting once you're dead?

Can spirits glide down more than one main street?
   Can they be here and also English Bay?
How is that son of yours? He was a treat
   Until Jack Daniels led the lad astray.
   You say he's staring at The Milky Way
And cursing you for "choosing Dad instead."

Poor blameless fool still at it night and day.
Does Oedipus stop haunting once you're dead?

L'Envoi

Attention, men! Please listen, if I may.
You must remove all mom-lust from your head.
     For when I asked her, Thelma answered "Nay!"
To Oedipus not haunting once you're dead.

Oak Creek Canyon

There is a place I go to still my mind
And offer thanks for yet another day.
It's where my deeper self gets more defined
And where the deer can hear me softly pray.
"God grant Serenity," I say aloud,
"And guide me with a sure and steady hand."
Three crows arrive. Then others join the crowd.
They cock their heads, as if to understand.
A trout swims up then darts away downstream,
Creating ribboned pathways in its wake.
Such moments are as fluid as a dream.
A water-cure for my most inner ache.
It's where each hour needs no ticking clock,
Where hope renews the heart on this, my rock.

Another Time, Another Tennis Court

I love myself enough today.
Despite those times I miss the ball.
I like the offbeat things I say.
The grunt before I cry "Bad call!"

Despite those times I miss the ball,
Despite my ragged shirt and shoes,
The grunt before I cry "Bad call!"
I'm fun. I'm free. I get to choose

My ragged shirt and running shoes
And who will keep me volleying.
I'm fun. I'm free. I get to choose
What's worth my gosh and gollying.

And who will keep me volleying.
I'm not as needy as before.
What's worth my gosh and gollying?
Good friends. They matter now, much more.

My swing goes wide. "Ya wanna bowl?"
I like the offbeat things I say.
Don't need a man to make me whole.
I love myself enough today.